COMPLETE RECORDINGS ILLUSTRATED
JILL GRIFFIN & ANDREW SPARKE

Essential Discographies No.108

APS PUBLICATIONS

NOTES

This short book simply collects the recorded work of Swedish pop phenomenon Abba and the solo work of the four group members. It has no grand aim except to introduce them to new listeners and save record buyers hours of research online in the form of a neat catalogue for the bookshelf.

COMPILER'S NOTE

The Eurovision Song contest held on 6th April 1974 in Brighton was a highlight of the year across the UK and in our house. Bets were being placed on who would win, as we vied for the best seats on the sofa to watch the contest, on our 26" colour television. I wanted Olivia Newton John to win and my parents, being Irish, were backing Tina Reynolds from Eire.

I remember watching Sven-Olef Walldoff dressed in an elaborate Napoleonic costume, left hand resting inside his jacket enter the stage to conduct the orchestra for Sweden who were contestants' number eight. He was confident, with an almost regal look, which really piqued my interest – this was going to be different!

With eyes glued to the screen the music commenced and Agnetha and Anni-Frid (known as Frida) ran down onto the main dais. I knew straight away that I was watching something life changing. That day they solidified my lifelong love of catchy popular music and the need to dance, whenever possible.

Their appearance was fun, but also glamorous and flamboyant and I adored it. Agnetha wearing a cobalt blue bomber jacket in velour fabric with matching satin pantaloons and sparkly cap; Frida in her swooshing, floor-sweeping skirt made of white and orange panels topped with a white jacket with large orange cuffs and collar; Bjorn and Benny matching their look.

For me Agnetha confidence and flowing blond hair stole the show, I wanted to be her! The fresh, awesome and intoxicating performance meant that no one was surprised when they won with a landslide victory.

Over the years, I bought all their albums and dressed as close to Agnetha as I dared. At weekends I'd be a party animal and could always be found dancing and singing around my handbag with girlfriends or partners. Never really being a drinker, my love of music meant I never left the dancefloor, especially if ABBA music was playing.

Recently I have watched 'Mama Mia' and 'Mama Mia Here We Go Again" repeatedly. After all these years I still know every word to all the songs and can only say 'Thank you for the Music' ABBA.

Jill Griffin

ABBA

ABBA was one of the most popular bands in history and Sweden's biggest ever pop group. The band was named from the initials of the four group members Agnetha Fältskog, Björn Ulvaeus, Benny Andersson, and Anni-Frid Lyngstad.

Their story began in 1966, when Bjorn Ulvaeus met Benny Andersson for the first time. At the time both were members of different bands, Bjorn the folk music group called the 'Hootenanny Singers' and Benny 'The Hep Stars', one of Sweden's biggest pop groups of the time for whom he played the keyboards.

They wrote their first song together in 1966 and by the end of the sixties they regularly partnered as composers. Benny left 'The Hep Stars', while the 'Hootenanny Singers' continued to produce music in a recording studio releasing their records on the Polar Music record label, owned by Stig Anderson. Stig famously went on to became ABBA's manager and helped write the lyrics to many of the hits of ABBA's early years.

In 1969, Bjorn (born 1945) and Benny (born 1946) met the two women who became the other half of the ABBA team and their wives. Agnetha (born 1950) was already a successful solo singer who had released her first single in 1967. She and Bjorn married in July 1971. Frida or Anni-Frid Lyngstad (born 1945 in Norway), started her recording career shortly before Agnetha and Frida and Benny married in October 1978.

From the start, the four group members contributed songs, instrumental backing and vocals and production work to the recordings they each made as solo or duo acts but in 1970 they decided combining their captivating voices would be an ideal option and together they put together the cabaret act Festfolk (which had the double meaning "engaged couples" and "party people").

Sadly, Festfolk failed, but in the spring of 1972 calling themselves Bjorn & Benny, Agnetha & Anni-Frid, they tried again. This time recording a song called 'People Need Love', they achieved some interest and the song became a popular hit in Sweden.

Delighted by their success, in 1973 they entered the Swedish selections for the Eurovision Song Contest with the song 'Ring Ring'. Finishing third, they released a single and album of the same name which competed in the Swedish charts for top positions while 'Ring Ring' became a hit in a number of other European countries too.

In 1974 the quartet again entered the Swedish selection process. This time 'Waterloo' took them all the way to the finals in England. They changed their name to ABBA, also the name of a Swedish Seafood company, which had been canning herring since the 1800s. Thankfully following legal negotiations they agreed to lend their name to the pop group and The Eurovision Song Contest 1974 turned out to be the most famous moment in ABBA history, and a landslide victory.

This discography records the fact that 'Waterloo' was only the start of a stunningly successful ten year lifespan garnering hundreds of millions of record sales until the members' respective divorces and the group's dissolution in 1982. That said ABBA's music remains omni-present to this day, not least due to the successful 'Mamma Mia' stage musical and films which hooked a new female generation of fans.

And now as ay 2021 there's a new album and tour after a forty year interlude. Proves you should never say *never again*.

ABBA ALBUMS

WATERLOO
(1974 Polar)

Waterloo
Sitting In The Palmtree
King Kong Song
Hasta Mañana
My Mama Said
Dance (While The Music Still Goes On)
Honey, Honey
Watch Out
What About Livingstone
Gonna Sing You My Lovesong
Suzy-Hang-Around
Waterloo *(English Version)*

RING RING
(1974 Polar)
Ring, Ring (Bara Du Slog En Signal)
Another Town, Another Train
Disillusion
People Need Love
I Saw It In The Mirror
Nina, Pretty Ballerina
Love Isn't Easy (But It Sure Is Hard Enough)
Me And Bobby And Bobby's Brother
He Is Your Brother
Ring, Ring (Engelsk Version)
I Am Just A Girl
Rock'n Roll Band

ABBA
(1975 Polar)
Mamma Mia
Hey, Hey Helen
Tropical Loveland
SOS
Man In The Middle
Bang-A-Boomerang
I Do, I Do, I Do, I Do, I Do
Rock Me
Intermezzo No. 1
I've Been Waiting For You
So Long

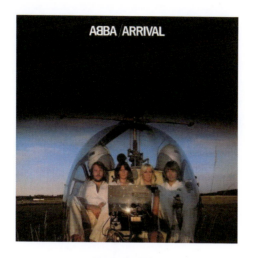

ARRIVAL
(1976 Polar)
When I Kissed The Teacher
Dancing Queen
My Love, My Life
Dum Dum Diddle
Knowing Me, Knowing You
Money, Money, Money
That's Me
Why Did It Have To Be Me
Tiger
Arrival

THE ALBUM
(1977 Polar)
Eagle
Take A Chance On Me
One Man One Woman
The Name Of The Game
Move On
Hole In Your Soul
"The Girl With The Golden Hair" – *3 Scenes from A Mini-Musical*
Thank You For The Music
I Wonder (Departure)
I'm A Marionette

VOULEZ-VOUS
(1979 Polar)
As Good As New
Voulez-Vous
I Have A Dream
Angeleyes
The King Has Lost His Crown
Does Your Mother Know
If It Wasn't For The Nights
Chiquitita
Lovers (Live A Little Longer)
Kisses Of Fire

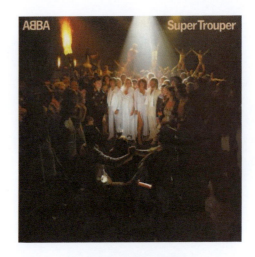

SUPER TROUPER
(1980 Polar)

Super Trouper
The Winner Takes It All
On And On And On
Andante, Andante
Me And I
Happy New Year
Our Last Summer
The Piper
Lay All Your Love On Me
The Way Old Friends Do

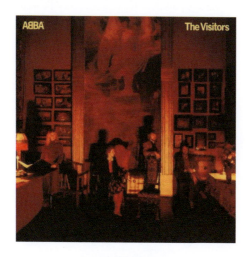

THE VISITOR
(1981 Polar)
The Visitors
Head Over Heels
When All Is Said And Done
Soldiers
I Let The Music Speak
One Of Us
Two For The Price Of One
Slipping Through My Fingers
Like An Angel Passing Through My Room

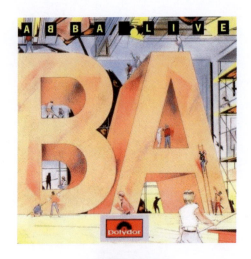

ABBA LIVE
(1986 Polar)
Dancing Queen
Take A Chance On Me
I Have A Dream
Does Your Mother Know
Chiquitita
Thank You For The Music
Two For The Price Of One
Fernando
Gimme! Gimme! Gimme! (A Man After Midnight)
Super Trouper
Waterloo
Money Money Money
Name Of The Game / Eagle
On And On And On

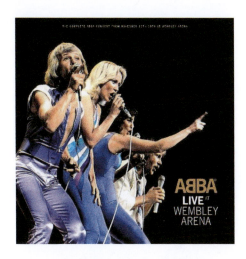

LIVE WEMBLEY ARENA
(2014 Polar)

Gammal Fäbodpsalm
Voulez-Vous
If It Wasn't For The Nights
As Good As New
Knowing Me, Knowing You
Rock Me
Chiquitita
Money, Money, Money
I Have A Dream
Gimme! Gimme! Gimme! (A Man After Midnight)
SOS
Fernando
The Name Of The Game
Eagle
Thank You For The Music
Why Did It Have To Be Me
Intermezzo No. 1
I'm Still Alive
Summer Night City
Take A Chance On Me
Does Your Mother Know
Hole In Your Soul
The Way Old Friends Do
Dancing Queen
Waterloo

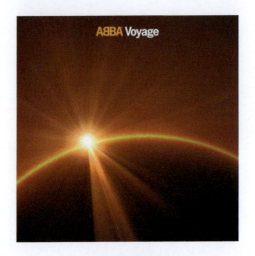

VOYAGE
(2021 Polydor)

I Still Have Faith In You
When You Danced With Me
Little Things
Don't Shut Me Down
Just A Notion
I Can Be That Woman
Keep An Eye On Dan
Bumblebee
No Doubt About It
Ode To Freedom

SINGLES

People Need Love/Merry-Go-Round *1972 Polar*
Ring Ring/She's My Kind Of Girl *1973 Polydor*
Waterloo (English Version/Watch Out *1974 Polar*
Honey Honey/King Kong Song *1974 Polar*
Hasta Manana/Watch Out *1974 Dig It International*
So Long/Hasta Manana *1974 RCA Victor*
Waterloo/Watch Out/Ring Ring/Rock 'N' Roll Band *1974 RCA Victor*
Ring Ring/Hasta Manaña *1974 Atlantic*
So Long/I've Been Waiting For You *1974 Polydor*
I Do, I Do, I Do, I Do, I Do/Rock Me *1975* Polar
I've Been Waiting For You /King Kong Song *1975 RCA Vistor - only released
as A-side in Australia and New Zealand*
SOS/The Man In The Middle *1975 Polar*
Mamma Mia/Intermezzo No. 1 *1975 Polar*
Fernando/Hey Hey Helen *1976 Polar*
Mamma Mia/Tropical Loveland *1976 Epic*
Dancing Queen/That's Me *1976 Polar*
Money, Money, Money/Crazy World *1976 Polar*
Knowing Me, Knowing You/Happy Hawaii *1977 Epic*
The Name Of The Game/I Wonder (Departure) *1977 Polar*
Take A Chance On Me/I'm A Marionette *1978 Polar*
Eagle/Thank You For The Music *1978 Polar*

Summer Night City/Medley: Pick A Bale Of Cotton/On Top Of Old Smokey/Midnight Special *1978 Polar*

Chiquitita/Lovelight *1979 Epic*

Does Your Mother Know/Kisses Of Fire *1979 Polar*

Voulez-Vous/Angeleyes *1979 Polar*

Gimme! Gimme! Gimme! (A Man After Midnight)/The King Has Lost His Crown *1979 Polar*

I Have A Dream/Take A Chance On Me (Live) *1979 Polar*

The Winner Takes It All/Elaine *1980 Polar*

Super Trouper/The Piper *1980 Polar*

One Of Us/Should I Laugh Or Cry *1981 Polar*

Head Over Heels/The Visitors *1982 Polar*

The Day Before You Came/Cassandra *1982 Polar*

Cassandra/The Day Before You Came *1982 Polar*

Under Attack/You Owe Me One *1982 Polar*

Waterloo (Swedish Version)/Waterloo (English Version) 2014 Polar

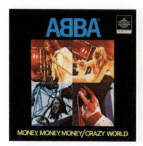

THE NAME OF THE GAME/I WONDER (Departure)

Dancing Queen
Dum Dum Diddle
Arrival
That's Me

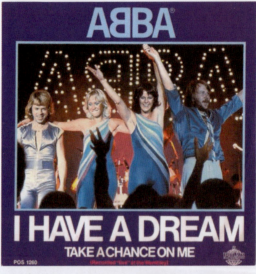

ABBA

I HAVE A DREAM

TAKE A CHANCE ON ME

POS 1260

Does Your Mother Know
Kisses Of Fire
From the New Album Voulez-Vous.

Eagle/Thank You For The Music

TAKE A CHANCE ON ME
I'M A MARIONETTE

SUPER TROUPER / ON AND ON AND ON

KNOWING ME, KNOWING YOU
HAPPY HAWAII (Early version of Why Did It Have To Be Me)

SOS
Man in the middle

AGNETHA FÄLTSKOG

AGNETHA FÄLTSKOG
(1968 Cupol)

Jag Var Så Kär
Jag Har Förlorat Dej
Utan Dej, Mitt Liv Går Vidare
Allting Har Förändrat Sig
Försonade
Slutet Gott Allting Gott
Tack Sverige
En Sommar Med Dej
Snövit Och De Sju Dvärgarna
Min Farbror Jonathan
Följ Med Mig
Den Jag Väntat På

AGNETHA FÄLTSKOG Vol 2
(1969 Cupol)

Fram För Svenska Sommaren
Lek Med Dina Dockor
Ge Dej Till Tåls
Skål Kära Vän
Glöm Honom
En Gång Fanns Bara Vi Två
Hjärtats Kronprins
Det Handlar Om Kärlek
Som En Vind Kom Du Till Mej
Senor Gonzales
Zigenarvän
Tag Min Hand Låt Oss Bli Vänner

SOM JAG ÄR
(1970 Cupol)
Som Ett Eko
När Jag Var Fem
En Sång Och En Saga
Tänk Va' Skönt
Ta Det Bara Med Ro
Om Tårar Vore Guld
Hjärtats Saga
Spela Vår Sång
Så Här Börjar Kärlek
Du Ska Minnas Mig
Jag Skall Göra Allt
Sov Gott Min Lilla Vän

NÄR EN VACKER TANKE BLIR EN SÅNG
(1971 Cupol)

Många Gånger Än
Jag Vill Att Du Skall Bli Lycklig
Kungens Vaktparad
Mitt Sommarland
Nya Ord
Jag Skall Inte Fälla Några Tårar
Då Finns Du Hos Mig
Han Lämnar Mig För Att Komma Till Dig
Kanske Var Min Kind Lite Het
Sången Föder Dig Tillbaka
Tågen Kan Gå Igen
Dröm Är Dröm, Och Saga Saga (Era Bello Il Mio Ragazzo)

ELVA KVINNER I ETT HUS
(1975 Cupol)

S.O.S
En Egen Trädgård
Tack För En Underbar, Vanlig Dag
Gulleplutt
Är Du Som Han?
Och Han Väntar På Mej
Doktorn
Mina Ögon
Dom Har Glömt
Var Det Med Dej?
Visa I Åttonde Månaden

NU TÄNDAS TUSEN JULELJUS (AGNETHA & LINDA)

(1981 Polar)

Nej Se Det Snöar

Bjällerklang

Nu Tändas Tusen Juleljus

Två Små Röda Luvor

Nu Står Julen Vid Snöig Port

Jag Såg Mamma Kyssa Tomten (I Saw Mommy Kissing Santa Claus)

När Juldagsmorgon Glimmar

Nu Har Vi Ljus Här I Vårt Hus

Tre Små Pepparkaksgubbar

Räven Raskar Över Isen

Vi Äro Musikanter

Hej Tomtegubbar

Jungfru Jungfru Kär

Nu Är Det Jul Igen

Hej Mitt Vinterland

Så Milt Lyser Stjärnan

Mössens Julafton

När Det Lider Mot Jul

WRAP YOUR ARMS AROUND ME
(1983 Polar)

The Heat Is On
Can't Shake Loose
Shame
Stay
Once Burned, Twice Shy
Mr. Persuasion
Wrap Your Arms Around Me
To Love
I Wish Tonight Could Last Forever
Man
Take Good Care Of Your Children
Stand By My Side

EYES OF A WOMAN
(1985 Polar)

One Way Love
Eyes Of A Woman
Just One Heart
I Won't Let You Go
The Angels Cry
Click Track
We Should Be Together
I Won't Be Leaving You
Save Me (Why Don't Ya)
I Keep Turning Off Lights
We Move As One

I STAND ALONE
(1987 WEA)

The Last Time
Little White Secrets
I Wasn't The One (Who Said Goodbye)
Love In A World Gone Mad
Maybe It Was Magic
Let It Shine
We Got A Way
I Stand Alone
Are You Gonna Throw It All Away
If You Need Somebody Tonight

KOM FOLJ MED I VÅR KARUSSEL (AGNETHA & CHRISTIAN)
(1987 WEA)

Karusellvisan
Våra Valpar
Mitt Namn Är Blom
Vattenvisan
Maskeradballen
Pelle Jöns
Tre Vita Råttor
Önskevisa
På Söndag
Smurferifabriken
Min Pony
Nicko Ticko Tin
Jag Vill Va' Som Du
Jag Är Kung
Alla Färger
Liten Och Trött

THE COLOURING BOOK
(2004 WEA)

My Colouring Book
When You Walk In The Room
If I Thought You'd Ever Change Your Mind
Sealed With A Kiss
Love Me With All Your Heart
Fly Me To The Moon
Past, Present And Future
A Fool Am I
I Can't Reach Your Heart
Sometimes When I'm Dreaming
The End Of The World
Remember Me
What Now My Love

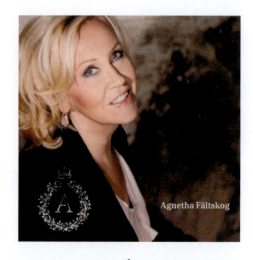

A

(2013 Universal Music Group)

The One Who Loves You Now
When You Really Loved Someone
Perfume In The Breeze
I Was A Flower
I Should've Followed You Home
Past Forever
Dance Your Pain Away
Bubble
Back On Your Radio
I Keep Them On The Floor Beside My Bed

SINGLES AND COMPILATION ALBUMS

AGNETHA FÄLTSKOG has an extensive catalogue of Swedish single releases and compilation albums which fall outside the remit of this Abba discography.

Agnetha Faltskog courtesy of Helge Øverås

ANNI-FRID LYNGSTAD

FRIDA
(1971 Columbia)

Tre Kvart Från Nu
Jag Blir Galen När Jag Tänker På Dej
Lycka
Sen Dess Har Jag Inte Sett'en
En Ton Av Tystnad
Suzanne
Allting Skall Bli Bra
Vad Gör Jag Med Min Kärlek
Jag Är Beredd
En Liten Sång Om Kärlek
Telegram För Fullmånen
Barnen Sover

FRIDA ENSAM
(1975 Polar)
Fernando
Jag Är Mej Själv Nu = Young Girl
Som En Sparv
Vill Du Låna En Man = The Most Beautiful Girl
Liv På Mars = Life On Mars
Syrtaki = Siko Chorepse Syrtaki
Aldrig Mej = Vado Via
Guld Och Gröna Ängar = Wall Street Shuffle
Ett Liv I Solen = Anima Mia
Skulle De' Va' Skönt = Wouldn't It Be Nice
Var Är Min Clown = Send In The Clowns

SINGLES AND COMPILATION ALBUMS

ANNI-FRID LYNGSTAD has an extensive catalogue of Swedish single releases and compilation albums which fall outside the remit of this Abba discography.

BENNY ANDERSSON & BJORN ULVAEUS

CHESS
(1984 Polydor)

Merano
The Russian And Molokov / Where I Want To Be
Opening Ceremony
Quartet (A Model Of Decorum And Tranquillity)
The American And Florence / Nobody's Side
Chess
Mountain Duet
Florence Quits
Embassy Lament
Anthem
Bangkok / One Night In Bangkok
Heaven Help My Heart
Argument
I Know Him So Well
The Deal (No Deal)
Pity The Child
Endgame
Epilogue: You And I / The Story Of Chess

BENNY ANDERSSON

KLINGA MINA KLOCKOR
(1987 Mono Music)
Inledningsvisa
Lottis Schottis
Födelsedagsvals Till Mona
Om Min Syster
Efter Regnet
Ludvigs Leksakspolka
Gladan
Långsammazurkan
Tittis Sång
Trolskan
Klinga Mina Klockor

NOVEMBER 1989
(Mono Music 1989)

Skallgång
Machopolska
Vals Efter Efraim Andersson
Sekelskiftesidyll
Dans På Vindbryggan
Stjuls
Tröstevisa
Målarskolan
Novell # 1
The Conducator
Stockholm By Night

CLASSICAL ALBUMS

BENNY ANDERSSON has contributed as composer to a number of classical releases and various cast recordings of his music for the musical CHESS which fall outside the remit of this ABBA discography.

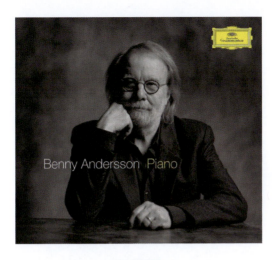

PIANO
(2017 Deutsche Grammophon)

I Let The Music Speak
You And I
Aldrig
Thank You For The Music
Stockholm By Night
Chess
The Day Before You Came
Someone Else's Story
Midnattsdans
Målarskolan
I Wonder (Departure)
Embassy Lament
Anthem
My Love, My Life
Mountain Duet
Flickornas Rum
Efter Regnet
Tröstevisa
En Skrift I Snön
Happy New Year
I Gott Bevar

COMPILATIONS

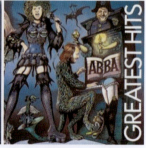

DVDs

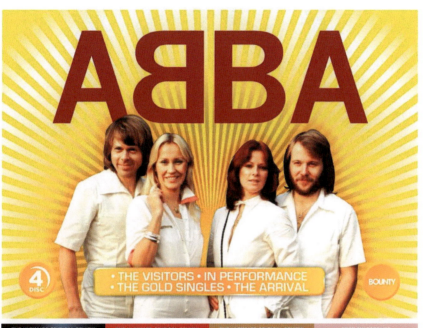

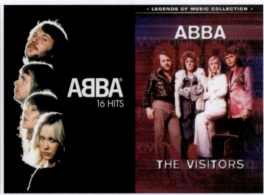

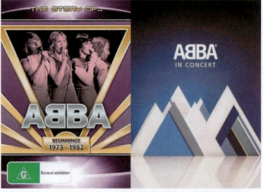

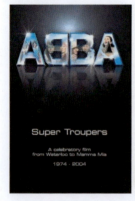

FURTHER READING

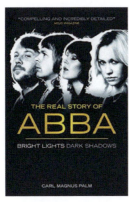

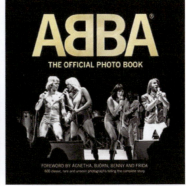

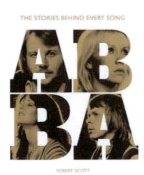

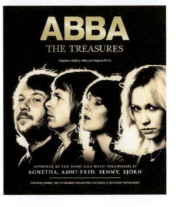

ESSENTIAL DISCOGRAPHIES FROM APS BOOKS

Printed in Great Britain
by Amazon

38671284R00027